From Ordinary
to
EXTRAordinary:
Success Begins Within

Mike Howard

For more information, contact:
MB Howard & Associates
PO Box 723574
Atlanta, GA 31139-0574
770-436-0638
SpeakerMBH@aol.com

ISBN: 1-59872-578-5

Printed in the US by Instantpublisher.com

Acknowledgments

This book is dedicated to the memory of my sister, Jacqueline Kinsey. Without her prayers, backing and continued belief in me, this book would not have been possible.

To my mother and father, Eva Mae and James Howard, for their love and support. They always believed in me, which made me believe in myself. Their persistence and their will to succeed are second to none.

To my sisters, Shirley May and Mildred Wilkinson: Your love inspires me to keep striving to be my best.

To my brother, Willie Howard: Thank you for your love and for being an example to me of what a man should be.

To all my nieces, nephews and cousins: You have provided me a support system and a foundation to succeed.

Lastly, thanks to all the members of BUY-Cobb, Inc., a mentorship and leadership organization. In particular, thank you to Don Johnson, Winston Strickland and Dr. Earl Holliday, for helping me develop my leadership skills and the greatness inside me.

About the Author

Mike Howard worked for 8½ years as a computer programmer for IBM (space shuttle division), and today he programs individuals for success through his speaking and training seminars as the president of MB Howard & Associates.

Mike was part of the IBM team at NASA's Mission Control Center during the 1986 space shuttle explosion and, as a speaker, he recounts how his team lived through one of the nation's lowest points. He uses the lessons he learned from that experience to deliver a message that inspires and moves people to higher levels of productivity and achievement. Mike will help your organization develop its flight plan for success or, individually, provide you with the motivation, inspiration and information to create a positive transformation in your life. His high-energy style will help you count down, lift off and propel yourself toward success.

Mike has traveled throughout this country making an impact on thousands of people with his message, training seminars, audiocassettes, CDs and motivational electronic newsletter. He has been featured on television and radio, talking about success and a winning attitude, and has been written about in local and national publications.

He delivers presentations about attitude, leadership, customer service, teambuilding and marketing. His clients include AT&T, Bristol-Myers Squibb, Cobb County government, Cobb County Public Schools, City of Atlanta government, Citizens Trust Bank, Corning, Equifax, Georgia Department of Labor, Georgia Power, Hartsfield-Jackson Atlanta International Airport, IBM, Kroger, Lucent Technologies, Sanofi Aventis, Social Security Administration, Sprint, SunTrust Bank and March of Dimes.

Table of Contents

Introduction

Your investment in time and money to read this book tells me that you want to begin achieving EXTRAordinary results in your life. You obviously know that success begins with quality information. Years ago, while I was working at IBM, a coworker named Stephen Strother gave me a self-help motivational tape that made a difference in all areas of my life and, because of that tape, I have been able to make a positive impact on many other lives. That's why I wrote this book—so you can grow and also so you can pass on the knowledge you receive from it.

I hope this small book will deliver big results. It is written in a format you can read easily and quickly. The last chapter contains exercises to help you get the best results. If you honestly work through the activities, they will work for you in your life.

As you read and apply this book, keep your eyes on your goals and desired results. There are thousands of people working to become successful whose names are still unknown but, within two years, five years, or maybe ten years, their names will be household names. Will yours be one of them? I believe it can be if you have a commitment to learn the essentials that will take you to the top.

Greatness begins in the mind with a vision. When Oprah Winfrey was following her dreams and working to learn the skills she needed for success, people probably said, "Oprah who?" The same question was likely asked of Bill Gates as well. Many people who are at the top of the ladder started at the bottom. Many at the front of the line started in the back. As you begin to read this book, you are at the starting point for creating an EXTRAordinary life. Good luck!

Chapter 1
Program Yourself for EXTRAordinary Achievement

Do you want to raise your level of personal and professional achievement? Attract more opportunities? Increase your income? Become a better employee or employer? If you answered yes to any of these questions, you have chosen the right book to help you achieve those results—in all areas of your life. Success begins with a thought and the ability to take action. Ordinary people can do EXTRAordinary things when they adopt the philosophy of a high achiever and consistently work to make that philosophy a habit.

The only difference between where you are today and where you will be tomorrow is the information you learn and the people you meet. We grow through people and knowledge. So begin to associate with people you can learn from, surround yourself with stimuli, and search for new information that will help you to grow and maximize your potential.

Here's my formula for EXTRAordinary results in life:

Information → Thoughts → Beliefs →

Attitude → Actions = Results

The information you receive determines your thoughts. Your thoughts impact your beliefs. Your beliefs affect your attitude. Your attitude influences your actions. And your actions yield the results in your life.

→ **Information** is knowledge gathered from study, experience, data or instruction. We receive messages from many sources—some good and some bad. The information we receive controls the results we get in our personal life, professional life, finances, relationships, and other parts of our lives. I once read that, if you read one hour a day for a year, you will become known in your community. If you read one hour a day for three years, you will become known across the nation. If you read one hour a day for five years, you will become known throughout the world.

→ **Thoughts** formulate in your mind based on the information you receive.

→ **Beliefs** are what you accept as truth.

→ **Attitude** is a complex mental state involving beliefs, feelings and values that cause you to act in certain a way.

→ **Action** is something you do or accomplish.

You can feed your mind positive information and thoughts, you can have a strong belief system and a winning attitude, but if you're not taking consistent action toward your goals, you won't achieve EXTRAordinary results and success. As you take action to move toward a goal, the movement is not only for the attainment of your goal but also for what you become as you move forward—the life lessons you'll learn and the skills you'll develop.

For example, when I took action to be published and written about in national magazines, the action helped develop other areas of my life as well. I learned about persistence because of the many rejections, improved my sales skills because I had to sell people on my knowledge, and learned to better understand those in charge because I had to think like the editors so I could write an article that would fit the style of their publications.

→ **Results** are the outcome of a particular action that leads to a concrete outcome.

As president and CEO of YOU INC., you need to regularly take inventory of your skills and assets. Rate yourself and identify ways you can improve.

- ✓ Do you have a positive attitude?
- ✓ Are your speaking skills top-notch?
- ✓ Do you understand people?
- ✓ Do you listen well?
- ✓ Are you an effective salesperson?
- ✓ Are you an effective marketer?
- ✓ Do you have strong self-discipline?
- ✓ Are you good at motivating people?
- ✓ Do you have, and use, leadership skills?
- ✓ Are you a competent networker?
- ✓ Are you good at teambuilding?
- ✓ Can you speed read?

To program yourself for success, you must monitor what you let enter your mind and work to override the negative programming that you hear every day. One study said that, by the time the average person is 18 years old, they have been told "No" or "You can't do that" about 150,000 times. You probably have heard one of the following:

- ✗ You're not smart enough.
- ✗ You don't have the knowledge to start a business.
- ✗ You don't have enough money.
- ✗ You're not a good communicator.
- ✗ You don't have the time or experience.

Unconsciously, we are programmed by other people and the information we hear. Have you ever wondered why you think or talk a certain way? It's because of what you've seen and heard throughout your life. For example, if a baby is born in Japan to Japanese parents, the child will grow up speaking fluent Japanese—unless someone takes the baby from the parents at an early age and raises the child in the United States. If that happens, the baby will grow up speaking English. He or she may look Japanese, but will speak English. We become like the people in our circle of influence.

Therefore, if you want to be EXTRAordinary, you must surround yourself with EXTRAordinary information and people. If you want to be a winner, you must surround yourself with winners. Construction workers say it's hard to build a house on a foundation that's only 50% complete. It's hard to build success on an incomplete foundation as well.

According to studies, the best time to read or listen to information that will allow you to achieve EXTRA-ordinary results is the first 30 minutes after you wake up in the morning and the last 30 minutes before you go to bed. These are the ideal times for your mind to accept new information and programming because it's operating between 8 and 13 wave cycles a second. This is known as the alpha state. Have you ever heard a song first thing in the morning and found yourself singing that song all day long? That is an example of being programmed while you're in the alpha state.

Many people, after a long day, listen to and/or watch the news before going to bed. That's not good. Studies show that what you hear 30 minutes before you go to bed is repeated in your subconscious mind about 16 times. Everything else repeats about 4 times!

From Ordinary to EXTRAordinary:

Instead of going to bed listening to how bad the economy or job market is, or how many people were murdered that day, go to sleep after reading or listening to something positive that will build you up, empower you and help you perform at an EXTRAordinary level. You may want to repeat some of the following thoughts before retiring tonight:

- ✓ If I am knocked down, I get back up, learn from my mistakes and move forward.
- ✓ The difference in the ordinary and EXTRAordinary individual is the ability to handle the challenges of life with a positive attitude.
- ✓ Knowledge creates opportunities.
- ✓ When my thoughts change, I change.
- ✓ I will seize every opportunity to develop the greatness inside me.
- ✓ If I can't find a job, I will create a job.
- ✓ I am reaching my true potential by consitently creating wealth in all areas of my life and in the lives of others.
- ✓ There is no such thing as a "money shortage," but there is an "idea shortage." Great ideas can generate money even when I don't have a dollar in my pocket.
- ✓ I am a multimillionaire whose money is being deposited into my bank account every day.

For 21 consecutive days, repeat positive thoughts before retiring for the night or starting your day.

8

Doing this will help you develop a new habit, and you will begin to see growth in your personal and professional life. You will attract new opportunities and feel better about yourself and your possibilities.

Even though you've committed to moving toward your goal and taking your life to the next level, you will sometimes face challenges and setbacks at work and at home. The key is to stay focused on where you're going, learn from your mistakes, and keep moving forward. What separates the ordinary from the EXTRAordinary is the ability to bounce back in the middle of adversity.

The explosion of the Space Shuttle Challenger in 1986 left the nation numb. That NASA team, of which I was a member, had to take responsibility and learn from our mistakes. We had to get up, move forward, and become better. Today, the space shuttle program is better and safer than it was in 1986. Because of the persistence and resilience of the team, the program was able to return and make many significant contributions to society, including weather satellites, satellite TV, cell phones, sophisticated intelligence systems, and advances in medicine.

The point is: Never give up. The knowledge that has brought you to this level is not enough to take you to the next. You must continue to learn and grow. If you want to achieve EXTRAordinary results, increase your sales, become a stronger team member, or grow into a better businessperson, that achievement begins with the seeds planted in your mind. To make it to the top and stay there, you must continue to fertilize your mind.

From Ordinary to EXTRAordinary:

Success Notes

Chapter 2
Thoughts for Success

This chapter is designed to give you the motivation, inspiration and information to create a transformation in your life. It contains quick and easy-to-understand information, success strategies, and thoughts and quotes that you can apply to all areas of your life.

I have spent years studying successful people and success principles. In this chapter, I have combined my own quotes with great thoughts from many of the top producers and achievers in the world. I have given credit to the quotes that could be tracked, and all biblical quotes are from the New International Version of the King James Bible.

Also, you will learn a little about the stories behind successful people and companies. Success always leaves a trail. I hope you will draw motivation, persistence and inspiration from these, and that the story behind the glory will give you an extra boost to keep pushing to become EXTRAordinary. Enjoy!

From Ordinary to EXTRAordinary:

Anyone can count the number of seeds in an apple, but it is impossible to count the number of apples in a seed.
— Dr. Robert H. Schuller

It's not until we begin to cultivate the seed that we begin to tap into its magic of producing apples. You have seeds of greatness and talents inside you, but you must work to develop them. — Denis Waitley, Seeds of Greatness

Success and excellence happen when you care enough to deliver your very best effort.

You can't jump to the top of a mountain. It is a step-by-step process.

No one gets through life without difficult times. You either are in a difficult time, just got out of a difficult time, or are headed toward a difficult time. Be ready to handle it and learn from it.

Without vision, we are blind to opportunity. — Unknown

Michael Dell attended college with plans to become a doctor. Because of his love of computers, he began selling them out of his dorm room. As Dell progressed, he developed an innovative approach: He sold computers directly to the consumer without going through retailers. Dell founded the Dell Corporation in 1984 with $1,000, and it's now a multibillion dollar corporation—the largest online commercial seller in the world.

During rapid change, denial, resistance, standing still, and not learning are the most dangerous courses of action.

Attitude: The good news is you don't have to buy it, but you do have to develop it. — *Keith D. Harrell*

Live each day as if it were your last, because one day it will be. — *Unknown*

After failing second grade because of dyslexia, Paul Orfalea was placed in a class for retarded students, but he didn't give up.

In September 1970, Orfalea, just out of college, borrowed enough money to open his first photocopy shop in Isla Vista, the campus community of UC at Santa Barbara. He called the store "Kinko's" after the nickname given to him by his college friends because of his curly, reddish hair.

This tiny Kinko's featured a single copier, an offset press, equipment for film processing and a small selection of stationery and school supplies. Not long after, the space became so crowded that the copier was occasionally rolled out onto the sidewalk for self-serve copies!

Kinko's had expanded to over 1,200 stores in the United States, Canada, the Netherlands, Japan, South Korea, Australia, the United Arab Emirates, China and Great Britain when it was acquired by FedEx Corporation in 2004 and became FedEx Kinko's.

From Ordinary to EXTRAordinary:

No one can stop you from reaching your goals and dreams unless you give them permission to do so. When people try to stop you, say, "Permission denied."

How you act will determine what you attract.

Don't wish on it — work on it.

Do all the good you can, by all the means you can, in all the ways you can, in all the places you can, at all the times you can, to all the people you can, as long as you can.
— Reverend John Wesley

You will have self-discipline or you will have regret.

Self-discipline is the ability to do what you must do, when you must do it, whether you feel like it or not.
— David Drewelow, The Practice of Discipline

Take ordinary things and do them in EXTRAordinary ways.

Problems are not placed in our lives to obstruct us but to instruct us. *— Unknown*

After graduating from law school, Sandra Day O'Connor could not get a job as a lawyer. A position as a legal secretary was the only job offered to her. She went on to become the first woman on the US Supreme Court.

14

Kindness is a language which the deaf can hear and the blind can read. — Mark Twain

What we do from 9 to 5 is survive. What we do after 5 is strive and get ahead. Instead of going home and watching television, go home and invest in your personal and professional growth.

Formal education will make you a living; self-education will make you a fortune. — Jim Rohn

Commit yourself to learning more than you are asked to learn.

It doesn't matter what happens to you. What matters is how you handle what happens to you. That is the difference that will make the difference. It will help you to stand when you don't understand.

John H. Johnson was born in a tin shack in Arkansas, but he had big dreams. Using his mother's furniture as collateral, he got a loan for $500 to launch the Johnson Publishing Company. He learned to deal with setbacks and misfortune by reading self-help books and biographies about successful people.

His persistence paid off. *Ebony* has been the number-one black-oriented magazine for more than 50 years. John Johnson was the first African-American to make the list of *Forbes* 400 richest people in America.

From Ordinary to EXTRAordinary:

Your mind responds and reacts to what you feed it.

The results you have achieved in your life are the summation of the information you have received, the thoughts and beliefs you have adopted, and the people you have met.

Tap into the power of OPK (other people's knowledge), OPE (other people's experiences) and OPN (other people's networks). Life is short and it's dangerous to live by trial and error.

As you reach your goals and become successful, always remain hungry and stay humble.

It may not look like it, but you're winning.

If you keep doing what you're doing, you will keep getting what you're getting.   *— Unknown*

Your life is not like a credit card. It has no limits.

Personal preparation precedes personal achievement.

Theodor Geisel's first book, *And to Think that I Saw It on Mulberry Street*, was rejected by almost every major publisher in the country. But Geisel remained persistent until one publisher believed in him. You know Geisel by his pen name: Dr. Seuss. Today, he is one of the top-selling children's authors in the world.

It's great to have the things that money can buy, but it is better to have the things that money can't buy: happiness, peace of mind, good health, love, etc.

When life knocks you down, you should always try to land on your back, because if you can look up, you can get up.
— Les Brown

Trying times are for trying and they produce triumphs.
— Unknown

Bloom where you are planted.   — Afghan proverb

A positive attitude invites positive results. A negative attitude invites negative results.

Life pays an exact wage. What you give to life, life will give back to you, and what you withhold from life, life will withhold from you.   — Unknown

---

As a junior at Yale, Fred Smith received a "C" for the term paper in which he outlined his concept for an express transportation company. The professor said it wouldn't work. After serving in the Marine Corps, Smith implemented the idea that he wrote about in that term paper by launching Federal Express. Offering overnight parcel deliveries and other courier services, FedEx quickly established itself as an integral part of the new, fast-paced global economy.

From Ordinary to EXTRAordinary:

Your life has limitless possibilities.

Prepare, plan and play to win!

People wishing for things to happen in their life will always be passed by those who are working to make things happen.

The future is yours. Plant it today. The seeds you plant today will shape your tomorrow. — *Unknown*

Winners accept feedback, learn from it, and self-correct.
— *Brian Tracy*

Build a reputation for always delivering more than is expected.

Tyler Perry, a New Orleans native, moved to Atlanta with $12,000 to put on a production of the stage play, *I Know I've Been Changed*. No more than 30 people showed up the entire weekend.

Later, Perry wound up homeless on several occasions, but he continued to hold on to his faith and belief in himself.

Because of his persistence, Perry went from being homeless to selling out theatres wherever he goes. He has become one of America's most successful playwrights, grossing nearly $100 million in theatre tickets, videos, DVDs and novelty items. His first feature film, *The Diary of a Mad Black Woman*, was a national success.

You can't build a reputation of being excellent by making excuses or by talking about what you intend to do.

Eliminate the word "can't" from your vocabulary. It is disempowering. It does not appear even once in the King James Bible.

How you dress will determine how you are addressed.

— *Unknown*

Business Success Rule: Your success is in direct proportion to what you do after you have done what you're expected to do.

— *Unknown*

Look out for big problems. They disguise big opportunities.

— *Unknown*

Six things that will affect your success in life:
1. The information you read
2. What you think about
3. What you believe
4. The information you listen to
5. What you watch
6. Your circle of friends and associates

He drew into a shell when his older brother was killed in World War II. To ease his pain, he began listening to the radio and dreamed of hosting his own radio show. This eventually led Dick Clark (America's oldest teenager) to start *American Bandstand.*

19

From Ordinary to EXTRAordinary:

Excellence has its price. If you want to see the world from the top of the mountain, you must equip yourself to make the climb.

Take a risk. The big fish are caught in the deep water.

Move from the safe zone into the faith zone.   *— Unknown*

You don't have to be great to get started, but you have to get started if you want to be great.   *— Unknown*

Your life will follow your thoughts.

Being defeated is often a temporary condition. Giving up is what makes it permanent.   *— Marilyn Vos Savant*

It was 1950 and Sam Walton had spent 5 years turning his first store, a five-and-dime Ben Franklin franchise in Newport, AR, toward profits. Then Walton had to sell the store because his landlord would not renew his 5-year lease.

Although at a low point, Walton did not dwell on his misfortune. He moved his family to Bentonville, AR, and rented a new store. This time, he had a 99-year lease. He made a commitment that this store would be bigger and better than his previous one.

Bigger and better is what he delivered. The new store was the start of what became the biggest retailer in the world: Wal-Mart Stores, Inc. Sam Walton turned a setback into a comeback.

Move out of your comfort zone. You can only grow if you are willing to feel awkward and uncomfortable when you try something new. — Brian Tracy

The secret to happiness is to count your blessings while others are adding up their troubles. — Unknown

Of all the attitudes we can acquire, surely the attitude of gratitude is the most important and by far the most life-changing. — Zig Ziglar

Ability is what you're capable of doing. Motivation determines what you do. Attitude determines how well you do it. — Lou Holtz

Opportunity is NOWHERE. (Do you see "now here" or "nowhere"?)

To go from ordinary to EXTRAordinary, you must be willing to stretch and move outside your comfort zone.

Some people try to become strong by pushing other people down, but the winners in life become stronger by pulling others up.

When Nathaniel Hawthorne was fired from his job, his wife urged him to write a book. She told him that she believed in him and knew he was a man of genius. Hawthorne used that "out-of-work" time to write one of the greatest masterpieces in American literature, *The Scarlet Letter.*

From Ordinary to EXTRAordinary:

A Poem to Help You Choose the Right Attitude

I am thankful for the taxes I pay each year because it means I have a job.

I am thankful for all the complaining I hear about our government because it means we have freedom of speech.

I am thankful for the mess I have to clean up after the party because it means I have been surrounded by friends.

I am thankful for the lawn that needs mowing, windows that need cleaning, and gutters that need repairing because it means I have a home.

I am thankful for the lady behind me in church who sings off-key because it means I can hear.

I am thankful for the alarm that goes off early in the morning because it means I am still alive.

I am thankful for the piles of laundry and ironing because it means my loved ones are nearby.

I am thankful for weariness and aching muscles at the end of the day, because it means I have been capable of working hard and using those limbs.

— Nancie J. Carmody

Find out what you want and go after it as if your life depends on it. Why? Because it does. — Les Brown

Procrastination is the assassination of motivation. — Unknown

Make the commitment to change your life. Take action TNT (today not tomorrow).

The seeds you sow in your mind will be manifested through your life.

Reading is to the mind what exercise is to the body. — Unknown

What you are is no indication of what you can become. — Jackie Kinsey

Patience, persistence and a positive attitude will always produce results. — Keith D. Harrell

---

You are unstoppable. Having a disability is no excuse for not reaching your dreams. These people had learning disabilities, but they didn't let the challenges stop them from pursuing greatness:

Harry Belafonte, actor, singer and civil rights activist
Cher, singer and actor
Jay Leno, comedian and talk-show host
Tom Cruise, actor
Whoopi Goldberg, actor and comedian

Beat your plowshares into swords, and your pruning hooks into spears. Let the weakling say, "I am strong."

— Joel 3:10

It's not what people say to you that will stop you from being successful, but what you say to yourself when they stop speaking. "I can't do that. I don't have the talent. I am not a good salesperson." Build yourself with empowering words: "I can, and I will, reach my goals. I am a true winner."

At the age of 6, Farrah Gray started carrying business cards proclaiming himself a "Future 21st Century CEO." Raised in the inner city of Chicago and living on public assistance, he had a driving desire to be successful. At 8, he cofounded the Urban Neighborhood Enterprise Economic Club, the forerunner of New Early Entrepreneur Wonders, which enlisted, educated and engaged at-risk youth by creating and developing legal ways for them to acquire additional income. By the time he was 14, he had made his first million dollars.

At 21, he received an Honorary Doctorate degree of Humane Letters from Allen University. Today, Gray is the youngest person to have an office on Wall Street (he also has one in Los Angeles). He is also the author of *Reallionaire,* which was nominated by NBC and *Publishers Weekly* Quill Awards in the category of Health/Self-Improvement.

Farrah Gray was an African-American teenager who rose from public aid to a successful business tycoon.

Fear is visualizing your limitations.

Knowledge, preparation and education build confidence and destroy fear.

A wealthy mindset precedes a wealthy wallet.

You are a product of your past, you represent the present, and you are the hope for the future.

Vision is the ability to see what others can't see and the capacity to see what others only dream. — Unknown

---

Dale Carnegie, self-help pioneer, failed in almost everything. He never graduated from college. He tried many careers, such as farming, acting, teaching, sales and journalism. They all failed. He lost most of his savings in the stock market crash of 1929.

His failures developed in him the desire to understand successful people and the process of becoming successful. Although Carnegie was an intensely shy man who feared public speaking, he inherently knew that success started with confidence, so he studied the subject and compiled his observations in his classic book, *How to Win Friends and Influence People*.

An estimated 50 million copies of his book have been sold in dozens of languages. Training courses in the Dale Carnegie method of public speaking have been taught nationwide to more than 7 million people.

From Ordinary to EXTRAordinary:

*Vision without action is a daydream; action without vision
is a nightmare.* — *Japanese proverb*

*Practice random acts of kindness. Each week, do something
especially kind for someone who does not expect it. Plant a
positive kernel of kindness and watch how life will give
back to you.* — *Conari Press*, Random Acts of Kindness

*You can make money [or success] or you can make excuses,
but you can't make both at the same time.*
— *Richard Carlson*, Don't Worry, Make Money

It is important that we learn to dream with our eyes open.
— *Melanie D. Geddes*
Learning to Dream with Your Eyes Open

*Big things are expected of us and nothing big ever came of
being small.* — *President Bill Clinton*

For as [a person] thinks within himself, so he is.
— *Proverbs 23:7*

Until 1905, Coca-Cola was marketed as a tonic.
During its first year in production, John
Pemberton, the druggist who invented the formula,
made only $50 (about 9 servings sold each day),
and it cost him over $70 in expenses, so the first
year was a loss. In 1887, another Atlanta
pharmacist and businessman, Asa Candler, bought
the formula from Pemberton for $2,300. Today, of
course, Coca-Cola is the best-selling soft drink in
the world.

26

What you say will determine your day. Speak your dreams. Breathe them and believe them. The more you speak them, the more they will become a part of your psyche and of your reality. Your words will create your world.

— Peter Sinclair

When working with others, remember that, if you don't respect, you won't progress. Everyone brings something to the team. Create an environment where others will be encouraged to be empowered.

When you find someone doing small things well, compliment them. This will encourage them to do big things well.

If you want to be EXTRAordinary, look at what others are doing and commit yourself to doing more and going the extra step.

What we are is God's gift to us. What we become is our gift to God.

— Eleanor Powell

Continuous learning is the fuel that drives everyone to find a better way of doing things. Training is not an expense but an investment in growth and renewal.

Sidney Poitier, Academy Award winning actor, was told after his first audition that he should stick to washing dishes.

From Ordinary to EXTRAordinary:

Treat everyone as if they are special because, in their eyes, they are. Hang an imaginary sign over their head that reads, "I care about you and you are the most important person in the world."

Learn the importance of listening. More learning takes place when we listen than when we talk. When you talk, you know what you know. When you listen, you know what you know and you will know what the other person knows. People with the ability to listen well position themselves for EXTRAordinary achievement.

The best job security is to perform your job better than anyone else can perform it. Always be willing to learn new things and keep a positive attitude. This will make you employable even if you are unemployed.

Some people don't ask questions because they don't want to be seen as weak. Others do ask questions because they want to become strong.

Achieve *comes before* **believe** *only in the dictionary. You must believe before you can achieve your goals.*

We shape our thoughts; then our thoughts shape us and our future. — Unknown

---

Dr. Robert Jarvik was rejected by 15 American medical schools. Later in his career, Dr. Jarvik invented the artificial heart.

Invest a percentage of your income in personal and professional growth. People spend more money on what goes on their head than what goes in their head. Many people will go to the barbershop or beauty shop twice a month, but won't buy one book a year for their personal and professional growth.

Lack of belief attracts failure.

A bad attitude is like a flat tire. You're not going anywhere until you fix it.   — *Allyson Wynne, Citibank*

When you succeed, it is because of what you know. When you fail, it is because of what you don't know. Make a point of learning something new every week that will improve your personal and professional growth.

The harder [you] work, the luckier [you] get.
                                            — *Samuel Goldwyn*

Thomas Edison claimed to have discovered a record number of ways not to build a light bulb, but he told a young reporter, "I have not failed at all. No, not once. I have successfully identified 5,000 ways that will not work. That body of work that you call failure, I call success, and it puts me 5,000 ways closer to finding the way that will work."

Eventually, Edison identified another 5,000 ways that didn't work before he was successful in finding the right formula for the light bulb.

From Ordinary to EXTRAordinary:

Your attitude will determine your action, your reactions, and how others react toward you. — Earl Nightingale

Do not be misled: Bad company corrupts good character. — 1 Corinthians 15:33

Expect to work hard. Easy is not an option.

Never say that something is impossible. In the 1960s, the following were not "possible" for public use:

Wireless cell phones
Satellite television
Navigational systems
DVD players
Caller ID
Internet
Fax machines

Only the limits of our imagination can control the boundaries of our reality. — Unknown

We get in life what we focus on receiving. Don't dwell on your weaknesses, capitalize on your strengths.

In 1955, Ray Kroc opened the first franchise of a new fast-food restaurant called McDonald's. The first day's sales were $366.12. In 1961, Kroc bought all rights to the McDonald's concept from the McDonald brothers for $2.7 million. Today, McDonald's sells over 1 billion hamburgers a day!

Winner vs. Loser

The Winner is always part of the answer;

The Loser is always part of the problem.

The Winner always has a program;

The Loser always has an excuse.

The Winner says, "Let me do it for you";

The Loser says, "That's not my job."

The Winner sees an answer for every problem;

The Loser sees a problem for every answer.

The Winner sees a green near every sand trap;

The Loser sees two or three sand traps near every green.

The Winner says, "It may be difficult but it's possible";

The Loser says, "It may be possible but it's too difficult."

Be a Winner.

— Unknown

From Ordinary to EXTRAordinary:

Use negative feedback as a navigational tool to make positive course corrections. — *Unknown*

Convert barriers into breakthroughs. It is when you are hit the hardest that you must not quit. Learn from all situations and stick to the task.

The only thing worse than being blind is having sight but no vision. — *Helen Keller*

You get the best effort from others not by lighting a fire beneath them, but by building a fire within. — *Bob Nelson*

There is no better way to become stronger than to reach down and pull others up. — *Unknown*

Quality products and quality service begin with quality thinking.

Ongoing study is the minimum requirement for success in any field. — *Denis Waitley*

Lucille Ball—five-time Emmy award winner, the first woman inducted into the Television Academy's Hall of Fame, recipient of a Genii Award, a Kennedy Center Honoree, a TV studio owner, a millionaire, and perhaps the most beloved of all television stars—was told by the head of a drama school to try another profession instead of acting.

Most people who fail in their dream fail not from lack of ability but from lack of commitment. Commitment produces consistent, enthusiastic effort that inevitably produces greater and greater rewards.   *— Zig Ziglar*

Where your knowledge stops, someone else's begins. We expand our mind by tapping into other people's knowledge.

*Taking action may not bring you success, but there is no success **without** action. Put together an action plan to reach your goals.*

I've learned that people will forget what you said, people will forget what you did, but people will never forget how you made them feel.   *— Maya Angelou*

Sometimes struggles are exactly what we need in our lives. If God allowed us to go through our lives without any obstacles, it would cripple us. We would not be as strong as we could have been. We could never fly!   *— Unknown*

The secret of success in life is for a man to be ready for his opportunity when it comes.   *— Benjamin Disraeli*

Cyclist Lance Armstrong finished LAST in his first professional race, but Armstrong bounced back— after a serious bout with cancer—and went on to set a record by winning the Tour De France seven consecutive times.

From Ordinary to EXTRAordinary:

Blessings in Disguise

I asked for strength

And God gave me difficulties to make me strong.

I asked for wisdom

And God gave me problems to solve.

I asked for prosperity

And God gave me brains and brawns to work.

I asked for courage

And God gave me dangers to overcome.

I asked for love

And God gave me troubled people to help.

I asked for favors

And God gave me opportunities.

I received nothing I wanted.

I received everything I needed.

My prayer has been answered.

— Unknown

Watch your thoughts; they become words. Watch your words; they become deeds. Watch your deeds; they become habits. Watch your habits; they become character. Character is everything. — Ralph Waldo Emerson

Growth is the ability to do that which is uncomfortable until it becomes comfortable.

Strength is not developed until weakness is disclosed.
— Unknown

In life, you miss 100% of the shots you never take.
— Wayne Gretzky

The great Babe Ruth was asked by a reporter, "What do you do when you get into a slump?"

Ruth paused, looked at him quizzically, and said, "A what?" The reporter replied, "A slump." Ruth answered, "I don't believe in slumps."

The reporter said, "Of course you've had slumps. Every baseball player has. You know, when you haven't hit very well or haven't had many home runs recently."

Ruth said, without hesitation, "Well, it's true that, when it's been a while since I've hit a home run, I do feel kinda sorry for the pitcher because I know, if I just keep swinging, it won't be long before they'll start disappearing over the fence again."

From Ordinary to EXTRAordinary:

What you know does not create success, but what you do consistently will create success.

Winners focus their attention on winning. Losers focus their attention on just getting by.

When given an opportunity or task, don't be afraid to accept the challenge. You should be more afraid not to accept the challenge. It is never about the challenge; it's about what you learn as you work through the challenge.

The list of Abraham Lincoln's failures before he was elected President is legendary. At 22, he lost his job as store clerk. At 23, he ran for the state legislature and was soundly defeated. At 26, his business partner died, leaving him with a large debt. The next year, he almost had a nervous breakdown when his best friend died.

At 29, after finally being elected to the House of Representatives, he was defeated in his bid to become House speaker. Two years later, he lost a bid for Presidential elector.

By 35, he had been defeated twice for Congress. At 39, after one term in Congress, he lost his reelection bid.

At 42, he was rejected as a federal land officer. At 45, he ran for the Senate and lost. At 47, he lost a bid for the vice-presidential nomination. At 49, he ran for the Senate again and lost again.

He was 51 when elected President. Thank heaven he persisted!

We expect perfection from others, but we ourselves are not perfect.

Don't be pushed by your problems. Be led by your dreams.
— *Unknown*

Promise big, but deliver bigger.

How far you go in life depends on your being tender with the young, compassionate with the aged, sympathetic with the striving, and tolerant of the weak and the strong. Because someday in life, you will have been all of these.
— *George Washington Carver*

Successful people have the power to elevate others toward success.

If you are not consistently learning, you are not growing. If you are not growing, you will never ignite your potential.

Until you believe in yourself, you won't believe in your future.
— *Unknown*

One of the most well-liked TV personalities in history, Oprah Winfrey, who went from rags to riches, says most of her success began after she started being consistent with a simple daily habit of writing down 3-plus things each day for which she is grateful.

From Ordinary to EXTRAordinary:

Plant a kernel of wheat and you reap a pint; plant a pint and you reap a bushel. Always the law works to give you back more than you give. — Anthony Norvell

Pass the gift of knowledge to your children. Your kids should not have to start where you started — they should start where you left off.

In life, you get what you seek. If you look for the good in a person, you will find it, but if you look for the bad, you will find that also. Compliment people on the good and magnify it.

If you [want to produce] for days, plant flowers. If you [want to produce] for years, plant tress. If you [want to produce] for eternity, plant ideas. — Unknown

Our imagination is the only limit to what we can hope to have in the future. — Charles Franklin Kettering

Jim Carrey, comedian and actor, used to look at the Hollywood lights and dream of success. One night in 1987, when the 25-year-old was struggling to reach his goal of becoming a box office hit, Carrey wrote himself a check for $10 million. He dated it Thanksgiving 1995 and added the notation, "For acting services rendered." By the time 1995 rolled around, Jim Carrey's asking price was up to $20 million per picture.

Learn from others who are wise and knowledgeable. Because life is short, you will not live long enough to figure it out on your own.

Be solution conscious: Focus 90% on the solution and 10% on the problem.

Men and women are limited not by the place of their birth, not by the color of their skin, but by the size of their hope.
— *John Johnson*

You must be willing to pay for your dreams with self-discipline, so you won't have to live with nightmares of regret. — *Dr. Stan Harris*

When you feel uncomfortable but take action anyway, you are growing.

Don't just be delivered from *the problem — be transformed* through *the problem.*

EXTRAordinary people will create *more opportunities than they find.* — *Unknown*

Walt Disney was fired by a Florida newspaper because he had no creative ideas. He went on to go bankrupt twice and have a nervous breakdown on his way to the Magic Kingdom.

39

From Ordinary to EXTRAordinary:

As you bless others, you will be blessed. According to Proverbs 11:25, "A generous man will prosper; he who refreshes others will himself be refreshed."

The Ethics Prayer
So far today, God, I've done all right. I haven't gossiped; haven't lost my temper; haven't been greedy, nasty, selfish or overindulgent. But in a few minutes, I'm going to get out of bed and I'm probably going to need a lot more help.
— Unknown

Tame the blame game. Assigning blame can be destructive to creativity, productivity and innovation.

The time is always right to do what is right.
— Dr. Martin Luther King, Jr.

The storms of life have a unique way of teaching us how to appreciate the sunshine.

As you take on a challenge, it builds the core of who you are even if you don't go through it perfectly.

Rejection comes to the big screen. The movie *Star Wars* was rejected by practically every movie studio in Hollywood, before 20th Century Fox finally decided to take a chance and produce it. *Star Wars* has gone on to be one of the largest grossing movies in film history.

40

*You can have everything in life that you want if you will
just help enough other people get what they want.*

— Zig Ziglar

*Listening allows you to connect with the heart of others by
using your ears. Look at the word "heart" and you will see
"ear" in the middle of it.*   *— Unknown*

*No man will make a great leader who wants to do it all
himself or get all the credit for doing it.*

— Andrew Carnegie

*A key to being EXTRAordinary is to value your reading
time, listening time and learning time three times as much
as your talking time. This philosophy will keep you on
course for greatness and continuous self-improvement.*

*Empower and teach others to lead. Don't be irreplaceable. If
you can't be replaced, you can't be promoted!*   *— Unknown*

*Pleasant words are like a honeycomb — sweetness to the
soul and health to the body.*   *— Proverbs 16:24*

*People learn not only from education but also through
imitation. Are your attitudes and actions worth imitating?*

The next time you are shopping in Macy's,
remember that R. H. Macy failed seven times
before his store in New York City succeeded. Now
Macy's is a major national retail store.

41

From Ordinary to EXTRAordinary:

Listen to wise advice and accept instruction, and in the end, you will be wise. — Proverbs 19:20

To be a winner and achieve EXTRAordinary results in life, you must RSVP:

R - Read
S - Study
V - Visualize
P - Perform well

Your mind is an incredible machine that can produce success. Whatever you program it to do, it has the capacity to accomplish.

Failure is only an event in your life — not a life.
— Unknown

The heart of the discerning acquires knowledge; the ears of the wise seek it out. — Proverbs 18:15

A happy person is not a person in a certain set of circumstances, but rather a person with a certain set of attitudes. — Hugh Downs

---

Cheers star Kirstie Alley lost 69 pounds in a little over a year by making up her mind to do so, setting a goal (70 pounds), exercising regularly, and following the rules of dieting. Persistence, dedication, and goals: the formula for success.

The road to success is dotted with many tempting parking places. — *Unknown*

Do not find fault; find a remedy. — *Henry Ford*

Life is short but, on the other hand, it is wide. Our success depends on how we utilize and maximize our potential while we travel through life.

Every failure is a blessing in disguise, providing it teaches some needed lesson one could not have learned otherwise. Most so-called failures are only temporary defeats.
                                                        –Unknown

---

Does age make a difference?

At the age of 3, Tiger Woods shot 48 for 9 holes at a Navy golf club in Cypress, California.

At the age of 13, Bill Gates wrote his first computer program. Bill and his classmate, Paul Allen, formed a programming group. At 19, Gates (and Allen) founded Microsoft.

At age 65, Colonel Harland Sanders drove around the country to sell his special chicken recipe. This was the start of what we know as Kentucky Fried Chicken.

Peter Mark Roget began compiling the huge concordance of synonyms and phrases with similar meanings when he was 60, and didn't finish until he was 72. His collection is known as *Roget's Thesaurus*.

From Ordinary to EXTRAordinary:

Live in the present but learn from the past. — *Unknown*

Our kids are not impressed by the time we work but they are impressed by the time we work with them.

*The three B's: If you **believe** in yourself and work to **build** yourself, you will **become** EXTRAordinary.*

What's in our head will determine if we get ahead.

Expand your network and you will expand your net worth.
— *Unknown*

Never be afraid to try something new. Remember that an amateur built the ark; professionals built the Titanic.
— *Unknown*

The longer you put off doing a job, the more difficult it gets. Do it now and stop procrastinating.

Roberto Goizueta, the late chairman and CEO of Coca-Cola, may be best remembered for using a mistake to increase shareholders' value from $4 billion to over $160 billion. When Goizueta introduced New Coke into the marketplace in 1985, he had the courage to admit he was wrong, reverse his decision, and reintroduce Classic Coke. That decision kept Coca-Cola on top. "We set out to change the dynamics of sugared colas in the United States, and we did exactly that—albeit not in the way we had planned," Goizueta said.

Learn to comprehend better by taking a speed-reading course. It will help you acquire more information quickly. If you want to change your output and achieve better results in life, improve the efficiency of your input.

Keep a success journal as a way to reflect on your past successes and boost your motivation. Write about any events that made you feel appreciated, a major accomplishment or milestone in your life, and awards or recognition. As you review your success journal, you will gain more appreciation for your progress and the gifts you bring to the universe. Success builds success. So keep reviewing your successes.

Develop the habit of reading about successful people. You will be inspired but, more importantly, you will learn the common characteristics that all successful people have. It is not just the success, but the story behind the success, that creates value for your personal and professional growth.

Hug people with your words.   *— Trinetta Love*

Dave Miller, a former partner in a restaurant in Jensen Beach, Florida, saw a necessity in his restaurant business. Because of the size and layout of the restaurant, they needed some way to let the waitresses know when the food was ready so they could speed up service. Miller coordinated with engineer Ron Halliburton to create a solution: the wireless pager. Today, not just servers but guests as well are accustomed to paging devices that alert them by beeping, vibrating or flashing.

From Ordinary to EXTRAordinary:

Learn to extract the life lesson from your mistakes. Take the lesson from the mistake and apply it to create a more successful life.

Form a support group with people who are motivated and committed to lifelong learning. Meet periodically to keep each other motivated and moving toward your goals.

Look into the mirror and get ruthlessly honest. Ask yourself the question, "Am I giving 100% and working to be the best that I can be?" If the answer is "No," you must take total responsibility for where you are. The good part is that, if you take responsibility, you are empowered with the ability to take your life to the next level. If you answered "Yes," you must continue to grow, because practice does not make perfect – it makes improvement.

What you don't know can, and will, hurt you. It will be used to hold you back in the game of life. – Unknown

A wise man will hear and increase learning, and a man of understanding will attain wise counsel. – Proverbs 1:5

Most Americans would never guess that Dr. Martin Luther King, Jr., earned a "C" in public speaking. He went on to win the Nobel Peace Prize and leave little doubt about his oratory prowess.

For God did not give us a spirit of timidity, but a spirit of power, of love and of self-discipline. — II Timothy 1:7

It is not who you know, but who knows you ... in a positive way, that will open up the doors of opportunity. — Unknown

[If] the question were asked, "Which nation is the strongest nation?" many Americans might say America, but the most powerful nation is imagination. Out of imagination is born great ideas. — Unknown

Learn from your "bad coworkers," "bad bosses" and "bad associates." Look for things they may be doing that are counterproductive and demotivating. Make note of these things and do whatever you can to eliminate them from your behavior.

Be strong and very courageous. Be careful to obey all the laws ...; do not turn from it to the right or to the left, that you may be successful wherever you go. — Joshua 1:7

The magic of the word "EXTRAordinary" comes in the first five characters: EXTRA. When you develop the habit of going the extra mile, you will become EXTRAordinary.

Alexander Graham Bell was actually trying to make a hearing aid for his mother and never did. But the telephone was a nice byproduct, don't you think?

From Ordinary to EXTRAordinary:

Success Creed

I have the equipment,
and today I make the commitment.
To give my best,
To be my best.

When the world says I can't, I say I can.
When the world says I won't, I say I will.

No one can stop me from reaching my goals
unless I give them permission to do so.
Every morning I wake up and say,
PERMISSION DENIED.

I give respect and I receive respect.
How I act will determine what I attract.
When I speak and open my mouth,
I tell the world who I am.

I watch my words; they become my thoughts.
I watch my thoughts; they become my beliefs.
I watch my beliefs; they become my habits.
I watch my habits; they become my actions.
I watch my actions; they become me.

I won't just talk about it, but I will BE about it,
Because actions speak louder than words.

Success is a choice and today I accept this creed to succeed.

— Mike Howard
Copyright 2006

A Wonderful Week

Many people go through life living for the weekend and wishing their lives away. What about the other five days? Stop wishing your life away and begin to live with excitement and enthusiasm.

When the birds wake up in the morning, they sing. When some people wake up in the morning, they complain. Know that many people wish they were in your shoes. If you have a day and your health, you have the potential to be EXTRAordinary. If you can get up, you have a chance to turn your dreams into reality. Remember:

> *Mondays are magnificent.*
> *Tuesdays are terrific.*
> *Wednesdays are wonderful.*
> *Thursdays are thrilling.*
> *Fridays are fabulous.*
> *Saturdays are superb.*
> *Sundays are spiritually fulfilling.*

*With this in mind, go out and **create** yourself a wonderful week!*

— Mike Howard
Copyright 2006

49

From Ordinary to EXTRAordinary:

Success Notes

Chapter 3
Your Flight Plan
for Success

If you want to achieve EXTRAordinary results in your life, you must be committed to making it happen. Success begins with your commitment. This chapter provides you with a guide and exercises for achieving EXTRAordinary results. It is now up to you to provide the effort and discipline to put the plan into action to develop a foundation for the success you want and deserve.

Find mentors and develop relationships with people who have achieved the level of success you are seeking. Talk to those people and learn about their failures along the way. Learn what they did to succeed. I've heard it said, "If you want to go somewhere, there is always someone who can show you how to get there." There are people you can talk to who hold the information and direction you need to succeed.

Make a wish list of 10 people you can meet who can give you information that will benefit your life. These can be people who have accomplished what you want to do or people who have experience in areas where you are striving to grow.

1.

2.

3.

4.

5.

6.

7.

8.

9.

10.

Do we hear more negative or positive information? The source can be radio, television, people, music or other media. The following exercise will help you monitor your input and thoughts.

List 10 positive statements you have recently heard:

1.

2.

3.

4.

5.

6.

7.

8.

9.

10.

From Ordinary to EXTRAordinary:

List 10 negative statements you have recently heard:

1.

2.

3.

4.

5.

6.

7.

8.

9.

10.

Influences

I was told in my early twenties that starting a business was very hard, and that it took money to make money. I heard that I should not even consider starting a business, because I would lose everything I had. For years, I believed that, and didn't even try to start my own business. I am glad that I overcame that negative programming.

List 5 examples of how negative input has influenced your life.

1.

2.

3.

4.

5.

From Ordinary to EXTRAordinary:

I was told by a successful businessperson to always deliver more than people expect because someone is always watching who can help you grow your business. That input has made a positive impact on my business and personal life. Many of my customers tell me that they brought me in to work with them because of my reputation for delivering 110%.

List 5 examples of how positive input has influenced your life.

1.

2.

3.

4.

5.

Write down how **negative information** you might hear in the future could impact your beliefs, your actions, and the results you want to achieve in life.

Write down how **positive information** you might hear in the future could impact your beliefs, your actions, and the results you want to achieve in life.

From Ordinary to EXTRAordinary:

Take inventory of the skills you need to become a peak performer and achieve better results. Evaluate your strengths and weaknesses, and be honest. As you develop yourself, you can turn weaknesses into strengths. Your success begins with a wealthy mindset. What skills do you need?

1. Speaking skills

2. Listening skills

3. Self-discipline

4. Time management skills

5. Ability to work with others

6.

7.

8.

9.

10.

We become like the people with whom we surround ourselves. List the 10 closest people to you. Are they a positive influence in your life or a negative influence?

1.

2.

3.

4.

5.

6.

7.

8.

9.

10.

From Ordinary to EXTRAordinary:

Some relationships allow us to grow and others hold us back. What are you learning, or have you learned, from the 10 people who are closest to you?

1.

2.

3.

4.

5.

6.

7.

8.

9.

10.

Success and happiness begin within. Whatever we focus on is magnified in our life. If we focus on our blessings and what we have, it will empower us and make us feel good about ourselves. This will affect our ability to pursue our goals and the attitude we project to others. You have more going *for* you than you have going *against* you.

While I was visiting someone at the hospital, I saw a man in intensive care with tubes coming out of his body. My friend, who was in the same room, said that the man had been admitted two months ago. I thought to myself that this patient would probably give anything to be blessed with good health, and I hoped he had taken the time to enjoy each moment of his life and be thankful for the things some of us take for granted.

Think about all the essentials you are blessed to have. From the things that money can't buy to the items money can buy, you are blessed. Develop an attitude of gratitude. Take a minute to write down the things you have to be thankful for:

1. My vision

2. The ability to walk

3. The ability to earn money

4. The pleasure of working inside with air conditioning

From Ordinary to EXTRAordinary:

5. The joy of working outside where I can enjoy nature

6. The fact that I get a vacation; some people don't

7. Family member(s) who love me

8. Good health

9. Somewhere to live

10.

11.

12.

13.

14.

15.

Write a Note of Thanks

Take a moment to think about the people who have made a positive impact on you, either directly or indirectly. You may have thought before about how thankful you are to have these people in your life. I want you to translate the thought into a letter of thanks. People are not inspired by our *thoughts*, but by our *words*.

List the people to whom you will send a note of thanks:

1. Name:

Why you want to thank them:

2. Name:

Why you want to thank them:

3. Name:

Why you want to thank them:

4. Name:

Why you want to thank them:

5. Name:

Why you want to thank them:

From Ordinary to EXTRAordinary:

Vision and Goals

Your success is tied to your vision for success. Since the mind thinks in pictures, you must have a vision of yourself succeeding. To help you create the vision, develop a Dream Book. In this book, you will write your vision, your goals, and what skills you need to develop in order to reach your goals. Insert pictures in your Dream Book of the accomplishments you want to attain: your dream house, your dream car, your dream check. The pictures will anchor you to your vision and your goal. Then you will work on the skills to attain these each day.

List your goals for the next **6 months**:

List 4 benefits you will enjoy as a result of reaching your 6-month goals:

1.

2.

3.

4.

64

List 4 obstacles you will have to overcome to attain your 6-month goals:

1.

2.

3.

4.

What information and knowledge will you have to get to accomplish your 6-month goals?

Identify the people, resources and organizations whose assistance you will need to accomplish your 6-month goals.

From Ordinary to EXTRAordinary:

List your goals for the **next year**:

List 4 benefits you will enjoy as a result of reaching
your 1-year goals.

1.

2.

3.

4.

List 4 obstacles you will have to overcome to attain your 1-year goals.

1.

2.

3.

4.

What information and knowledge will you have to get to accomplish your 1-year goals?

Identify the people, resources and organizations whose assistance you will need to accomplish your 1-year goals:

From Ordinary to EXTRAordinary:

List your goals for **3-5 years** from now:

List 4 benefits you will enjoy as a result of reaching your 3-5 year goals.

1.

2.

3.

4.

List 4 obstacles you will have to overcome to get your 3-5 year goals.

1.

2.

3.

4.

What information and knowledge will you have to get to accomplish your 3-5 year goals?

Identify the people, resources and organizations whose assistance you will need to accomplish your 3-5 year goals.

From Ordinary to EXTRAordinary:

Taking Responsibility

Take responsibility for where you are in life. Your actions have determined the results you have achieved. Motivation *gets* you going, but the habit of constantly taking positive action will *keep* you going in the right direction. What actions, if you took them immediately, could have the greatest impact on the results you are achieving in life?

1.

2.

3.

4.

5.

Keys to Success

Success leaves a trail in all areas of life. Search for the "diamonds of life." It's important that we learn from successful people who are in and out of our circle of influence. When we stand on the shoulders of giants, we become stronger. When we learn from successful people who have more knowledge than we have, it makes us smarter and accelerates our success. Identify people in the following areas and ask them these questions:

Family: What are the keys to having a close and loving family?

Name:
His/her keys to family success:

1.

2.

3.

Name:
His/her keys to family success:

1.

2.

3.

Relationships: What are the keys to having good relationships?

Name:
His/her keys to relationship success:

1.

2.

3.

Name:
His/her keys to relationship success:

1.

2.

3.

Financial: What are the keys to financial success?

Name:
His/her keys to financial success:

1.

2.

3.

Name:
His/her keys to financial success:

1.

2.

3.

From Ordinary to EXTRAordinary:

Business: What are the keys to success in business?

Name:
His/her keys to business success:

1.

2.

3.

Name:
His/her keys to business success:

1.

2.

3.

Spiritual: What are the keys to having a strong spiritual base?

Name:
His/her keys to a strong spiritual base:

1.

2.

3.

Name:
His/her keys to a strong spiritual base:

1.

2.

3.

From Ordinary to EXTRAordinary:

Health: What are the keys to optimal health?

Name:
His/her keys to optimal health:

1.

2.

3.

Name:
His/her keys to optimal health:

1.

2.

3.

Action Plan
for EXTRAordinary Productivity

Identify 3 things you will START doing today to become more productive:

1.

2.

3.

Identify 3 things you will STOP doing today that are hindering your productivity:

1.

2.

3.

From Ordinary to EXTRAordinary:

Success Thoughts

The results you are achieving are a product of your thoughts, which are impacted by the information you have received through the years. List 10 thoughts or quotes you will use to empower yourself. Say these to yourself early in the morning and/or right before you go to bed at night. Change your list every 30 days.

1.

2.

3.

4.

5.

6.

7.

8.

9.

10.

Success Learning

What are you doing to learn information that will position you for opportunities in the future? If you are not preparing yourself for opportunity, you won't be ready when it comes along, and it will pass you by.

Become a student of life. Commit to reading self-help books at least 15-30 minutes each day. Reading increases your chance for success. You can learn ideas from others and immediately convert them to your own success formula. Learn more so you can earn more. The information to succeed is available and within your reach, but you must be proactive by getting the information and applying it to your life. Your input will determine your income.

How many self-help books have you read in the past year?

Recommended books:

Live Your Dreams, Les Brown

See You at the Top and *Over the Top*, Zig Ziglar

Chicken Soup for the Soul, Jack Canfield and Mark Victor Hansen

The 21 Indispensable Qualities of a Leader, John C. Maxwell

The Power of Positive Thinking, Dr. Norman Vincent Peale

Attitude is Everything, Keith Harrell

How to Win Friends and Influence People, Dale Carnegie

Reallionaire: Nine Steps to Becoming Rich from the Inside Out, Farrah Gray and Fran Harris

Think and Grow Rich, Napoleon Hill

Business Leaders and Success, Investor's Business Daily and William O'Neil

Psycho-Cybernetics, Maxwell Maltz

Attitude 101: What Every Leader Needs to Know, John C. Maxwell

One Small Step Can Change Your Life, Robert Maurer

Think Like a Winner!, Walter Doyle Staples

What self-help books will you read (one a week) that will speed up your personal and professional growth?

1.

2.

3.

4.

5.

If you don't have time to read, you can listen to self-help audios in your car. A study at a university in California discovered that, if you drive an average of 12,000 miles a year and listen to self-help audios for 3 years, you will have the equivalent of 2 years of college. By using this technique, I have learned information that has tripled my income. While stuck in traffic, I have accelerated my personal and professional growth.

The information I have learned about marketing, sales and public relations has allowed me to be published and written about in local and national publications. When people ask, "How did you get so lucky to get written about in that magazine?" I tell them it wasn't luck. It was the principles I learned while riding in my automobile. I believe "a commute is a terrible thing to waste."

You can also listen to self-help audios while riding the bus, exercising or cleaning your home.

Recommended audios:

Lead the Field, Earl Nightingale

The Psychology of Achievement, Brian Tracy

How to Build a Network of Power Relationships, Harvey Mackay

Speak to Win, Bert Decker

From Ordinary to EXTRAordinary:

What self-help audios will you start listening to next week that will speed up your personal and professional growth?

1.

2.

3.

4.

5.

Success Notes

Success Notes

Order Form

☐ Please send me _____ copies of *From Ordinary to EXTRAordinary: Success Begins Within* (book) at $19.95 plus $3.95 for US shipping.

☐ Please send me _____ copies of *This Way to Success* (CD) at $19.95 plus $3.95 for US shipping.

**Call 770-436-0638 for information on volume order discounts, volume shipping and international shipping.

☐ Please sign me up for your FREE monthly electronic newsletter, *Motivational Minutes with Mike Howard.*

Name: _____

Company: _____

Street Address: _____

City/State/ZIP: _____

Phone: _____

Email: _____

Payment: ___ Amex ___ Visa ___ MasterCard ___ Check
___ Money Order

Mail to:
MB Howard & Associates
PO Box 723574
Atlanta, GA 31139